COLLEGE FOOTBALL
POWERHOUSE PROGRAMS

Sports Illustrated KIDS

SPORTS ILLUSTRATED KIDS BOOKS

Editor Sachin Shenolikar
Senior Art Director Edward Duarte
Writers: Sarah Braunstein, André Carter, Gary Gramling
Assistant Photo Editor/Designer: Gina Houseman
Reporting Intern Alan Garcia

Copyright 2008
Time Inc. Home Entertainment

Published by Sports Illustrated Kids Books

Time Inc.
1271 Avenue of the Americas
New York, New York 10020

ISBN 10: 1-60320-796-1
ISBN 13: 978-1-60320-796-6

SIK Books is a trademark of Time Inc.

TIME INC. HOME ENTERTAINMENT

Publisher Richard Fraiman
General Manager Steven Sandonato
Executive Director, Marketing Services Carol Pittard
Director, Retail & Special Sales Tom Mifsud
Director, New Product Development Peter Harper
Assistant Director, Brand Marketing Laura Adam
Associate Counsel Helen Wan
Senior Brand Manager, TWRS/M Holly Oakes
Design & Prepress Manager Anne-Michelle Gallero
Book Production Manager Susan Chodakiewicz
Brand and Licensing Manager Alexandra Bliss

Special Thanks: Glenn Buonocore, Margaret Hess, Suzanne Janso,
Dennis Marcel, Robert Marasco, Brooke Reger, Mary Sarro-Waite,
Ilene Schreider, Adriana Tierno, Alex Voznesenskiy

We welcome your comments and suggestions about SIK Books. Please
write to us at:
SIK Books
Attention: Book Editors
PO Box 11016
Des Moines, IA 50336-1016

If you would like to order any of our hardcover Collector's Edition books,
please call us at 1-800-327-6388.
(Monday through Friday, 7:00 a.m.– 8:00 p.m. or Saturday, 7:00
a.m.– 6:00 p.m. Central Time).

Welcome to *College Football Powerhouse Programs*, your guide to the top 20 schools in college football history. The teams were selected by the editors and writers of SI KIDS magazine. We took into account the history and reputation of each school, the championships it's won, and the superstars it's produced. All the statistics in this book were up to date as of the start of the 2008 season.

CONTENTS

USC

Overstocked with talent, the Trojans are always in the hunt for a national championship

With a team like USC to root for, it's no problem that Los Angeles doesn't have an NFL franchise. The Trojans have been competitive for decades and are in another golden age under coach Pete Carroll. USC has gone 76–14 in Carroll's seven seasons. In that span, they have lost only one game by more than seven points. With a shot at a championship nearly every season, USC attracts the nation's top recruits — which means the Trojans's future is always looking bright in sunny Southern California.

Mark Sanchez

SCHOOL STATS

- **First Year:** 1888
- **National Championships:** 9
- **Bowl Appearances:** 46
- **All-Time Record:** 754–302–54
- **NFL Players Produced:** 416

PLAYERS TO WATCH IN 2008

◄ JOE McKNIGHT

Sophomore, Tailback, 6', 180 lbs. McKnight is on track to be the next big star of the USC running game. In 2007, he had 903 total yards and four touchdowns, even though he saw most of his action as the team's punt returner. He finished the season averaging 8.4 yards per carry and was named to *The Sporting News* Pac-10 all-freshman first team. McKnight's ability as a receiver adds to his all-around package. He had three games with at least 100 all-purpose yards, including the 2008 Rose Bowl, in which he finished with 206.

■ REY MAUALUGA

Senior, Linebacker, 6' 3", 250 lbs. Maualuga led the Trojans in tackles (79) and was the defensive MVP of the Rose Bowl last season. He was first-team All Pac 10 in the past two seasons. Maualuga has a good shot to win the Butkus Award, given to the nation's top linebacker.

■ MARK SANCHEZ

Junior, Quarterback, 6' 3", 225 lbs. Sanchez started in place of an injured John David Booty for three games in 2007. He went 2–1, with 66 completions for 642 yards and seven TDs. Sanchez was named the '08 starter in April, but he will have pressure from Mitch Mustain, a transfer from Arkansas.

TOP TROJANS IN THE NFL

► **CARSON PALMER** *Quarterback, Cincinnati Bengals.* The 2007 Pro Bowl MVP was second in the AFC in completions (373) and yards (4,131) and fifth in touchdown passes (26). He became the fifth-fastest QB in NFL history to throw for 100 touchdowns (59 games).

■ **REGGIE BUSH** *Running Back, New Orleans Saints.* Bush was a dazzling rookie for the Saints in '06 (1,523 total yards). He set the NFL rookie record for catches by a running back with 88. In '07, he led the Saints in rushing yards (581).

■ **MARCUS ALLEN** *Hall of Fame Running Back.* Allen was named NFL Rookie of the Year in 1982 and the league's MVP in 1985. He became the first player in NFL history to have 10,000 rushing yards and 5,000 receiving yards in his career.

USC HISTORY

The Trojans Rush to Success

On November 14, 1888, the USC football team played its first game and earned its first victory, 16–0, over the Alliance Athletic Club. The team was known as the Methodists and then the Wesleyans, before adopting the Trojan as its mascot in 1912. One of the most famous teams in USC history was the 1932 national championship team known as the Thundering Herd. The team went 10–0 and scored 201 points while allowing only 13. In later years, USC would be called Tailback U for producing five Heisman Trophy-winning running backs. A USC player has won the Heisman Trophy seven times — tied with Notre Dame and Ohio State for the most of any school. It also has produced more Pro Football Hall of Famers (11) than any other college.

OKLAHOMA

It's loud and clear: The Boomer Sooners are one of the most dominant programs in college football

Oklahoma's football program is a machine that keeps churning out amazing teams. The Sooners have had 30 double-digit-win seasons — the most of any school. They've won their conference title a whopping 41 times and can claim 144 All-America players, including four Heisman Trophy winners. Oklahoma has been the Number 1 team in the Associated Press's weekly national poll 95 times since 1936. That ties Notre Dame for the most Number 1 rankings of any school.

Sam Bradford

SCHOOL STATS
- **First Year:** 1895
- **National Championships:** 7
- **Bowl Appearances:** 41
- **All-Time Record:** 779–295–53
- **NFL Players Produced:** 272

PLAYERS TO WATCH IN 2008

◄ JUAQUIN IGLESIAS,

Senior, Wide Receiver, 6'1", 201 lbs. Iglesias is quarterback Sam Bradford's favorite target. He led Oklahoma with 68 catches and 907 receiving yards in 2007. Iglesias also excels as a kickoff returner. He was 16th in the nation with an average of 28.5 yards a return.

■ SAM BRADFORD,

Sophomore, Quarterback, 6'5", 213 lbs. Bradford had no trouble adjusting to the college game as a freshman last season. He set the NCAA freshman record for touchdown passes with 36 — seven more than the previous record. He also led the nation in passer efficiency (176.53). The strong-armed Bradford twice tied the school record for TD passes in a game (5). He was accurate too, completing 24 straight pass attempts, two shy of the NCAA record. Bradford will be a Heisman Trophy favorite in 2008.

■ AUSTON ENGLISH,

Junior, Defensive End, 6'3", 257 lbs. Even though he missed three games with a right ankle injury, English still had 9.5 sacks last season. Now fully recovered, he has the strength and speed to be among the nation's leaders in QB takedowns.

OKLAHOMA HISTORY

Always in Title Contention

Here's a record that's hard to break: The Sooners had a 47-game winning streak from October 10, 1953, through November 9, 1957. No other modern Division I-A college football team has ever won more than 35 straight. But Oklahoma's excellence has continued beyond that stretch. Hall of Fame coach Barry Switzer led the Sooners to 157 wins and an .837 winning percentage from 1973 through 1988. And coach Bob Stoops has expertly guided Oklahoma's recent success. The team has played in three of the past eight national championship games and last won the title at the Orange Bowl in 2001. Oklahoma is also famous for its fight song, *Boomer Sooner*, and its tradition of the Sooner Schooner, a pony-drawn wagon that charges onto the field after every Sooners score at home games.

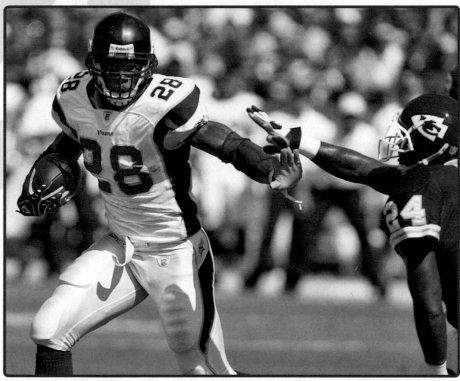

TOP SOONERS IN THE NFL

▲ **ADRIAN PETERSON**, *Running Back, Minnesota Vikings.* Peterson made quite the splash as an NFL rookie in 2007. He set the league's single-game rushing record (296 yards) against the San Diego Chargers in November.

■ **TOMMIE HARRIS**, *Defensive Tackle, Chicago Bears.* A two-time first-team All-America at Oklahoma, Harris has continued to dominate opponents in the pros. He's made it to two Pro Bowls.

■ **ROY WILLIAMS**, *Safety, Dallas Cowboys.* Williams, who won the Jim Thorpe Award as the nation's top collegiate defensive back in 2001, has played in five straight Pro Bowls.

NOTRE DAME

Luck of the Irish? No way! South Bend has been home to some of the most talented teams ever.

Notre Dame's 3–9 record in 2007 was a disappointment, but it didn't tarnish the reputation of the Blue and Gold. The Fighting Irish have the second-most victories (824) of any team in the Football Bowl Subdivision and have won or shared 11 national championships. A Notre Dame player has won the Heisman Trophy seven times, tied with USC and Ohio State for the most of any school. Fighting Irish players have gone on to big-time success in the pros, too. Ten Golden Domers have been elected to the Pro Football Hall of Fame. This year's Irish will work toward reclaiming that winning tradition.

Jimmy Clausen

SCHOOL STATS
- **First Year:** 1887
- **National Championships:** 11
- **Bowl Appearances:** 28
- **All-Time Record:** 824–278–42
- **NFL Players Produced:** 452

PLAYERS TO WATCH IN 2008

◄ **JAMES ALDRIDGE,** *Junior, Halfback, 6'0", 222 lbs.* Aldridge will be a major factor on offense this season. As a sophomore, he started five games and led the Irish in rushing yards (463). He has impressive speed and the strength to break tackles. He's also a good receiver out of the backfield.

■ **JIMMY CLAUSEN,** *Sophomore, Quarterback, 6'3", 207 lbs.* As a high school senior in 2006, Clausen was named the Parade co-Player of the Year and *USA Today*'s Offensive Player of the Year. In '07, he became Notre Dame's starter in the second game — the earliest a freshman QB has started for the Irish. He completed 138 passes for 1,254 yards, seven touchdowns, and six interceptions in his first college season.

■ **GOLDEN TATE,** *Sophomore, Wide Receiver, 5'11", 188 lbs.* Tate has the speed, explosiveness, and talent to be a deep threat. He spent the majority of the 2007 season as a kick returner, but of his six receptions as a wideout, four were for more than 20 yards.

NOTRE DAME HISTORY

A Wealth of Gridiron Riches

No school's football history is as rich as Notre Dame's. In the school's 1913 game against Army, the Irish became the first team to use the forward pass as part of their offense. From 1918 through '30, Notre Dame had a record of 105-12-5 while winning three national titles under legendary coach Knute Rockne. The 1924 squad was known for the backfield called The Four Horsemen. And of course there's the story of Daniel (Rudy) Ruettiger in 1975. The 5'6" Irish fan made the scout team but had never played in a game. In Notre Dame's final home game of the '75 season, coach Dan Devine put Rudy in for two plays as a defensive end and he sacked the QB. Teammates chanted "Ru-dy! Ru-dy!" as they carried him off the field.

TOP FIGHTING IRISH IN THE NFL

■ **JULIUS JONES,** *Running Back, Seattle Seahawks.* Jones is one of six Irish running backs to rush for more than 3,000 yards in an NFL career. He had his best pro season in 2006, with 1,084 yards on 267 carries for the Dallas Cowboys.

▲ **RYAN GRANT,** *Running Back, Green Bay Packers.* Grant ran for 770 yards and eight TDs in the final eight games of the '07 season. He rushed for a Packers postseason-record 201 yards in Green Bay's win over the Seattle Seahawks.

■ **JOE MONTANA,** *Hall of Fame Quarterback.* Montana was known for his come-from-behind victories. He led the San Francisco 49ers to four Super Bowl titles and made eight Pro Bowls. He became the fifth QB to pass for more than 40,000 yards in a career and retired with 273 TDs.

ALABAMA

Brimming with tradition, the Crimson Tide keeps bowling over opponents

From legendary coach Paul (Bear) Bryant, to the chants of "Roll Tide," Alabama has a rich college football tradition. The Crimson Tide has won more bowl games (31) than any other program, and the team ranks sixth all time for the most victories in FBS (formerly Division I-A) history. After falling on hard times earlier this decade, the program is on the rise again thanks to the arrival of coach Nick Saban in 2007.

John Parker Wilson

SCHOOL STATS
- **First Year:** 1892
- **National Championships:** 10
- **Bowl Appearances:** 55
- **All-Time Record:** 788–311–43
- **NFL Players Produced:** 237

PLAYERS TO WATCH IN 2008

■ JOHN PARKER WILSON,

Senior, Quarterback, 6' 2", 213 lbs.
Mr. Consistency should be Wilson's nickname. In 2007, he broke his own single-season school records for completions (255), passing yards (2,846), and touchdown passes (18). Among all Southeastern Conference players, he ranked fourth in total offense (226.9 yards per game). Wilson also became just the third Crimson Tide quarterback with two or more seasons of at least 2,000 yards of total offense (2,846).

▶ RASHAD JOHNSON,

Senior, Safety, 6', 187 lbs. A first-team All-SEC selection in 2007, Johnson tied for the conference lead with six interceptions and led the Crimson Tide with 81 tackles. He was named Alabama Co-Defensive Player of the Week five times.

■ ANDRE SMITH,

Junior, Offensive Tackle, 6' 5", 340 lbs.
Smith is on the preseason watch list for the Outland Trophy, which is awarded to the best interior lineman in the nation. He has played 26 straight games at left tackle. Last season, he was a first team All-SEC selection and earned the Jacobs Blocking Trophy as the best offensive lineman in the SEC.

TOP CRIMSON TIDE IN THE NFL

▶ **SHAUN ALEXANDER**, *Running back, Formerly of the Seattle Seahawks.* Alexander is one of the most productive running backs in history. In 2005, he set the NFL single-season record for touchdowns (28) and was named league MVP. Since 2000, he ranks second among all players in total touchdowns scored (112).

■ **DeMECO RYANS**, *Linebacker, Houston Texans.* Ryans was named the AP Defensive Rookie of the Year in 2006 and earned his first Pro Bowl selection last season.

■ **JOE NAMATH**, *Hall of Fame quarterback.* Broadway Joe was one of the NFL's most exciting players in the 1960s and the 70s. He is best known for leading the New York Jets to an upset win over the Baltimore Colts in Super Bowl III.

ALABAMA HISTORY

A Powerful Dynasty Keeps On Rolling

The birth of the Crimson dynasty occurred on November 11, 1892. Then known as the Crimson White, Alabama beat a team that was made up in part of high school kids from Birmingham, Alabama, 56–0. After a one-year absence in 1898, Alabama's program began a steady rise to college football's mountaintop. Led by coach Wallace Wade, the 1925 Crimson Tide finished with the school's first undefeated and untied season and won the first of 10 national championships. The start of the 1958 season ushered in the Bear Bryant Era. From 1958 through '82, Alabama won six national championships and 12 SEC titles. Bryant retired as the winningest coach in college football history (323 victories). In 1992, led by coach Gene Stallings, the Crimson Tide upset Miami in the Sugar Bowl to win its 10th national championship.

MICHIGAN

Playing in front of massive crowds, the Wolverines know how to put on an awesome show

Brandon Minor

N o team packs 'em in quite like Big Blue, which has boasted an attendance of at least 100,000 in 208 consecutive home games. And the Wolverines rarely disappoint their fans: They haven't had a losing season in 41 years. The school has the most victories (869) and the highest winning percentage (.746) of any team in college football history. The Wolverines also have won nine national titles.

SCHOOL STATS
- **First Year:** 1879
- **National Championships:** 9
- **All-Time Record:** 869–286–36
- **NFL Players Produced:** 312

PLAYERS TO WATCH IN 2008

■ BRANDON MINOR,
Junior, Running Back, 6'1", 214 lbs.
Minor is the front-runner to fill the hole left by running back sensation Mike Hart, who is now in the NFL. Minor had 385 rushing yards in 2007, second-most on the team.

■ OBI EZEH,
Junior, Linebacker, 6'2", 247 lbs.
Ezeh was fifth on the team in tackles (68) and was named to *The Sporting News* Freshman All–Big Ten team in 2007. The Wolverines are counting on him to have an even bigger season in '08.

▶ BRANDON GRAHAM,
Junior, Defensive End, 6'2", 270 lbs.
In 2007, Graham led the Wolverines in sacks (8.5) and was second on the team in forced fumbles (3). His best performance came against Notre Dame on September 15, when he had 3.5 sacks. A powerful player with a quick burst off the line, Graham will be a top candidate for the 2008 Ted Hendricks Award, given to the nation's best defensive end. His play will be a huge key to the success of an inexperienced Wolverines defense.

TOP WOLVERINES IN THE NFL

▶ TOM BRADY,
Quarterback, New England Patriots. A part-time starter in college, Brady blossomed once he reached the NFL. He's led the New England Patriots to three Super Bowl titles and holds the NFL record for most touchdown passes in a season (50).

■ BRAYLON EDWARDS, *Wide Receiver, Cleveland Browns.* Edwards won the Biletnikoff Award as the nation's best college receiver in 2004. He had a breakout season for the Cleveland Browns in '07 (1,289 yards and 16 TDs).

■ STEVE HUTCHINSON, *Offensive Lineman, Minnesota Vikings.* A five-time Pro Bowler, Hutchinson has opened running lanes for Adrian Peterson (Vikings) and Shaun Alexander (formerly of the Seattle Seahawks).

MICHIGAN HISTORY
Thrilling Through the Ages
The Wolverines have had only 11 losing seasons since 1892. In legendary coach Fielding Yost's first five seasons (1901–05), Michigan went 55-5-1 and outscored opponents 2,821-42. Michigan's star-studded history has included former U.S. president Gerald Ford, who played center for the Wolverines on their national championship team in 1933. Michigan also has three Heisman Trophy winners. The last Wolverine to win was cornerback Charles Woodson in 1997. Woodson became the first defensive player since 1949 to win the award. In November, coach Lloyd Carr retired after 13 seasons. New coach Rich Rodriguez, who led West Virginia to three straight double-digit-win seasons, will try to lead Michigan to its first national title since 1997.

OHIO STATE

The Buckeyes have the second-most wins (443) of any team in Big Ten conference history. Ohio State is also the only Big Ten school to play in a national championship game since the start of the BCS in 1998. Though the Buckeyes lost in the big game in each of the past two seasons, the school has a lot to be proud of. Ohio State has a strong reputation for building tough teams, having won 18 bowl games and 32 conference championships. Surely, more are on the way.

After two straight national-title game defeats, can the Buckeyes break through and win the big one?

James Laurinaitis

SCHOOL STATS

- **First Year:** 1890
- **National Championships:** 7
- **Bowl Appearances:** 39
- **All-Time Record:** 798–302–54
- **NFL Players Produced:** 359

PLAYERS TO WATCH IN 2008

◀ CHRIS WELLS

Junior, Running Back, 6'1", 237 lbs. Despite battling ankle and wrist injuries in 2007, Wells ran for 1,609 yards and scored 15 touchdowns. Nicknamed Beanie, Wells is the leader of a deep group of running backs. He finished in the top three in the Big Ten in net yards (1,609), rushing touchdowns, and yards per game (123.8) last season. He was Ohio State's team MVP last year.

■ JAMES LAURINAITIS

Senior, Linebacker, 6'3", 240 lbs. The two-time All-America was awarded the Butkus Award as the nation's best linebacker in 2007, after winning the Bronko Nagurski Trophy as the nation's best defender in '06. Laurinaitis was also named Big Ten Defensive Player of the Year in '07, when he finished with 121 tackles, five sacks, and two interceptions.

■ TODD BOECKMAN

Senior, Quarterback, 6'4", 240 lbs. Despite struggling in the final three games of 2007, the job of starting QB for the Buckeyes is Boeckman's to lose. He will be challenged by freshman Terrelle Pryor, the top high school QB recruit in the nation. Even though Boeckman is not especially fast, he has a strong arm and finished last season with 2,379 passing yards and 25 TDs.

OHIO STATE HISTORY

The Team and the Band Rock to the Tune of Success

In 1899, only nine years after football became a varsity sport at Ohio State, the Buckeyes notched their first undefeated season (9-0-1). That marked the beginning of a legacy of success. The Buckeyes have won seven national championships. Six Buckeyes have won the Heisman, including running back Archie Griffin, the only two-time winner in college football history. In addition to great football, Ohio State also provides great entertainment. The band's tradition of spelling 'Ohio' on the field — and the privilege of dotting the "i" — is a highlight of every home game.

TOP BUCKEYES IN THE NFL

■ **A.J. HAWK** *Linebacker, Green Bay Packers.* Hawk was the Packers' first-round draft pick in 2006. As a rookie, he led Green Bay in tackles (119) and was third in NFL Defensive Rookie of the Year voting. He had another strong year in 2007, finishing with 105 tackles.

◀ **MIKE VRABEL** *Linebacker, New England Patriots.* Last season, Vrabel tied for sixth in the NFL in sacks with 12.5. In '06, he was a key player on a Pats defense that allowed only 14.81 points per game, a franchise record. Vrabel is also an occasional end-zone target for QB Tom Brady. In his 11-season career, Vrabel has caught eight passes, all of them for TDs.

■ **SANTONIO HOLMES** *Wide Receiver, Pittsburgh Steelers.* Entering his third NFL season, Holmes has become an important playmaker in the Steelers offense. In 2007, he became one of QB Ben Roethlisberger's favorite receivers and ended the season with 942 yards and eight TDs.

U MIAMI

The Hurricanes have been blowing away their competition for more than two decades

Starting in the early 1980s and continuing through the turn of this century, the University of Miami changed the game of college football. Known for their brash attitude and athletic players, the Hurricanes were never dull to watch. And the program's emphasis on speed over size changed the way other programs recruited players. From 1983 through 2001, Miami won five national championships under four head coaches, including three in a five-year span.

Graig Cooper

SCHOOL STATS

- **First Year:** 1926
- **National Championships:** 5
- **Bowl Appearances:** 31
- **All-Time Record:** 545–304–19
- **NFL Players Produced:** 268

PLAYERS TO WATCH IN 2008

◄ JAVARRIS JAMES,

Junior, Running Back, 6', 214 lbs. The running game is in James's genes — his cousin is NFL star Edgerrin James, also a former Hurricane. Last season, Javarris was second on the Hurricanes in rushing yards (582). In 2006, his 802 rushing yards were the second-most by a true-freshman in Miami history.

■ ANTHONY REDDICK,

Senior, Safety, 6', 208 lbs. After missing the entire 2007 season with a left knee injury, Reddick will return as one of the best safeties in the nation. He has 80 tackles, one sack, one forced fumble, and one interception in 18 career games. Reddick also excels on special teams and has blocked two punts.

■ GRAIG COOPER,

Sophomore, Running Back, 6', 202 lbs. Last season, Cooper was an honorable mention freshman All-America. He led the Hurricanes in rushing yards (682) and averaged 5.5 yards per carry. His 116-yard performance against Marshall in September was the best-ever debut by a Hurricanes running back. Overall, his 682 yards were the third-highest total by a Miami true freshman. Cooper also led the Hurricanes in total touchdowns with five (four rushing, one receiving).

MIAMI HISTORY

A Program Blossoms into An NFL Factory

Miami football has been around since 1926, but it wasn't until 1983 that the program began its rise to greatness. Led by freshman quarterback Bernie Kosar, the Hurricanes upset Nebraska 31–30 in the Orange Bowl to win their first national championship. Four years later, Number 2–ranked Miami knocked off top-ranked Oklahoma in the Orange Bowl and completed its first undefeated season. Three more national titles followed, in 1989, 1991, and 2001. The '01 team will go down as one of the greatest in college football history. Its roster included future NFL stars Willis McGahee, Clinton Portis, Jonathan Vilma, Jeremy Shockey, and Vince Wilfork. Since '83, 47 Hurricanes have been taken in the first round of the NFL draft, and the school has produced a first-round-pick for a record 14 straight years.

TOP HURRICANES IN THE NFL

◄ ED REED, *Safety, Baltimore Ravens.*

As a senior in 2001, Reed was the Big East Co-Defensive Player of the Year. In 2004, he was named NFL Defensive Player of the Year.

■ FRANK GORE, *Running Back, San Francisco 49ers.*

Gore, who averaged 9.1 yards a carry as a freshman at Miami, leads all NFC running backs in rushing yards (2,797) since 2006.

■ ANDRE JOHNSON, *Wide Receiver, Houston Texans.*

A co-MVP of the 2002 Rose Bowl, in which Miami won its fifth national championship, Johnson is a two-time NFL Pro Bowler. He led the league in receptions (103) in 2006 and had eight TDs in nine games in '07.

FLORIDA STATE

A long string of fantastic seasons made the Seminoles the brightest spot of the Sunshine State

The garnet and gold colors of Florida State represented excellence in the 1980s and the '90s. Led by Bobby Bowden, college football's third-winningest coach, the Seminoles devastated their opponents with high-scoring offenses and won national championships in 1993 and '99. The '99 team became the first in the history of the Associated Press poll to hold the Number 1 ranking in the nation for an entire season. In 1985, the Seminoles began an NCAA record run of 11 straight bowl game victories. And from 1987 through 2000, they had 14 straight Top 5 finishes in the final AP poll.

Myron Rolle

SCHOOL STATS
- **First Year:** 1902
- **National Championships:** 2
- **Bowl Appearances:** 37
- **All-Time Record:** 373–119–4
- **NFL Players Produced:** 217

PLAYERS TO WATCH IN 2008

◀ DREW WEATHERFORD,
Senior, Quarterback, 6′3″, 216 lbs.
Weatherford ranks third in school history in passing yards and eighth in career completions and touchdown passes. He also does a great job of protecting the football. Last season he set team and ACC single-season records for most consecutive passes without an interception (270).

■ MYRON ROLLE,
Junior, Defensive Back, 6′2″, 218 lbs.
Rolle has been a tackling machine since his freshman season. He has averaged 72 tackles per season, and *The Sporting News* named him its 2006 ACC Defensive Rookie of the Year.

■ GREG CARR,
Senior, Wide Receiver, 6′6″, 210 lbs.
Carr's 25 touchdown catches are tied for eighth in ACC history. He is one of only six players in Florida State history with at least 30 receptions in three straight seasons.

TOP SEMINOLES IN THE NFL

▶ **ANQUAN BOLDIN**, *Wide Receiver, Arizona Cardinals.* Boldin played quarterback, wide receiver, and even returned kickoffs and punts as a Seminole. In the NFL, he ranks sixth among all players in receptions (413) since 2003.

■ **DERRICK BROOKS**, *Linebacker, Tampa Bay Buccaneers.* Brooks was a first-team All-America in 1994. The 10-time Pro Bowler was the NFL Defensive Player of the Year in 2002.

■ **ANTONIO CROMARTIE**, *Cornerback, San Diego Chargers.* Cromartie was an All-ACC selection in 2004. He led the NFL in interceptions last season with 10.

FLORIDA STATE HISTORY
Two Famous Coaches Bring National Acclaim to FSU

From 1905 through 1946, Florida State College was an all-female school. In 1947, one year after turning coed and changing its name to Florida State University, the school debuted its first football team. Under the offensive innovation of coach Bill Peterson, who is credited with the development of the "hot receiver" in blitz situations, the Seminoles began gaining recognition in the 1960s. But it wasn't until the hiring of coach Bobby Bowden in 1976 that Florida State skyrocketed to college football's elite. In order to build his program, Bowden took the Seminoles on the road, where they beat some of the giants of the sport. In 1993, Bowden and the Seminoles won their first national championship, led by Heisman Trophy–winning quarterback Charlie Ward. Six years later, led by another star QB in Chris Weinke, the 'Noles won their second national title.

NEBRASKA

A legendary program looks to recapture its glorious past

Nebraska's dominance has spanned over four decades. The school twice won back-to-back national championships (1970–1971 and 1994–1995) and had an FBS-record 33 straight seasons with at least nine wins (1969–2002). Nebraska's 808 wins rank fourth in FBS history, and the school has had nine undefeated seasons. Three Cornhuskers have won the Heisman Trophy (Johnny Rodgers, Mike Rozier, and Eric Crouch). The team has fallen on hard times recently, going 5–7 in 2007. New coach Bo Pelini will look to get the program back on the winning track this year.

Marlon
Lucky

SCHOOL STATS

- **First Year:** 1890
- **National Championships:** 5
- **Bowl Appearances:** 44
- **All-Time Record:** 808–333–40
- **NFL Players Produced:** 309

PLAYERS TO WATCH IN 2008

◄ **LARRY ASANTE,** *Junior, Safety, 6'1", 210 lbs.* Asante transferred to Nebraska from Coffeyville Community College in Kansas. As a sophomore at Nebraska last year he started 10 of 12 games and was second on the team in tackles (78). He was named honorable mention All-Big 12.

■ **MARLON LUCKY,** *Senior, Running Back, 6', 215 lbs.* In 2007, Lucky set the Nebraska record for receptions in a season (75). He had the most catches of any running back in the nation. With 84.9 rushing yards per game last season, Lucky is also the top returning rusher in the Big 12 Conference.

■ **JOE GANZ,** *Senior, Quarterback, 6'1", 210 lbs.* Ganz was Nebraska's backup for the first eight games of the 2007 season, but played great after starter Sam Keller got hurt. Ganz set Nebraska's single-game records for passing yards (510) and touchdowns (7). He ended the season with three straight games of at least 400 yards passing. Prior to that, there had been only two other 400-yard passing days in Nebraska history.

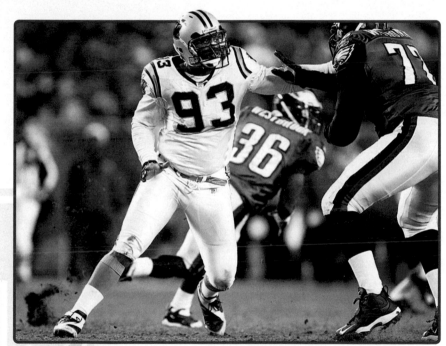

NEBRASKA HISTORY
Steamrolling Opponents with the I-Formation

Nebraska's football program began in 1890, when it beat the Omaha YMCA. The opponents got tougher after that, and the Huskers slowly grew into a college football dynasty. In 1969, the team started using the I-formation at the suggestion of assistant coach Tom Osborne. They won back-to-back national championships in 1970 and '71. Osborne took over as head coach in 1973. Things peaked for the Huskers in the 1990s, when they won three national championships — all with undefeated seasons. The 1995 squad is arguably the greatest in the history of college football. It went 12–0, and averaged a mind-blowing 52.4 points and 399.8 rushing yards per game.

TOP HUSKERS IN THE NFL

▲ **MIKE RUCKER,** *Former Carolina Panthers Defensive End.* Rucker helped the Huskers to national titles in 1995 and '97. He is second on the Panthers' all-time list for career sacks (52.5) and tackles (496).

■ **AHMAN GREEN,** *Running Back, Houston Texans.* Green's 8,751 career rushing yards are sixth among active players. As a Green Bay Packer from 2000-06, he became the franchise's all-time leader in yards from scrimmage (10,870).

■ **ROGER CRAIG,** *Legendary Running Back.* In 1988, the San Francisco 49er became the first NFL player to have at least 1,000 rushing and receiving yards in the same season. He was the 1988 NFL Offensive Player of the Year and helped the Niners win three Super Bowls in the 1980s.

TEXAS

The Longhorns are the pride of a state where football is king

Don't mess with Texas. The Longhorns have the third-most FBS victories of all time (820 wins in 115 seasons). They are one of four college football teams to reach the 800-victory mark. Texas has won four national championships (its most recent title came in 2006.) From Earl Campbell to Vince Young, Texas is known as a hotbed of superstars. Who will be the next Longhorn great?

Quan Cosby

SCHOOL STATS
- First Year: 1893
- National Championships: 4
- Bowl Appearances: 46
- All-Time Record: 820–316–33
- NFL Players Produced: 241

PLAYERS TO WATCH IN 2008

◄ COLT McCOY
Junior, Quarterback, 6'3", 210 lbs.

McCoy, the 2006 national freshman of the year, is already tied for the eighth-most career victories in Texas history (20 wins in 26 starts). He has a career passer rating of 148.9 and a 66.4 completion percentage — the best among all Texas QBs with at least 700 attempts. A two-time Longhorns co-MVP and two-time bowl game offensive MVP, McCoy holds the school record for most touchdowns in two consecutive seasons (51). He has thrown TD passes in 23 of his 26 games and had at least two TDs in 15 of those games.

■ QUAN COSBY
Senior, Wide Receiver, 5'11", 205 lbs.

Get ready for the Cosby show. Quan is seventh on Texas's all-time receptions list (120) and has caught at least one pass in 31 straight games, 16 shy of the school record. Cosby is also an impressive return man. His 1,381 return yards are second-best in school history.

■ BRIAN ORAKPO
Senior, Defensive End, 6'4", 260 lbs.

Named Big 12 defensive freshman of the year in 2005, Orakpo has developed into one of the nation's best ends. He is incredibly quick off the ball, with 90 tackles and 10.5 sacks in 35 career games.

TEXAS HISTORY

Toppling the Giants

The Longhorns are known for their exciting victories. In the team's first game on November 30, 1893, it beat the Dallas Football Club, 18–16. The Longhorns went on to lose only one game in their first three seasons. Texas won its first national title in 1963. In the 1970 Cotton Bowl, the Longhorns converted two fourth-and-two plays to defeat powerhouse Notre Dame. In 2006, more than 30 years after their last national championship, the Longhorns came from behind to defeat USC, 41–38, in the Rose Bowl. That game ended the Trojans' 34-game winning streak.

TOP LONGHORNS IN THE NFL

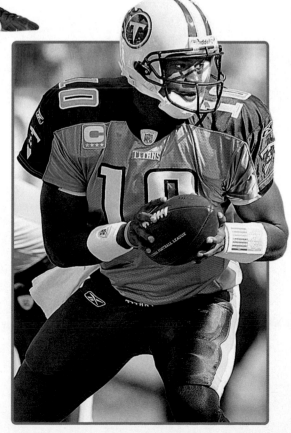

► **VINCE YOUNG**, *Quarterback, Tennessee Titans.* Young was drafted third overall by the Tennessee Titans in 2006. That year, he became the first rookie QB in the Super Bowl era to rush for 500 yards in a season.

■ **ROY WILLIAMS**, *Wide Receiver, Detroit Lions.* At Texas, Williams set career school records for receptions, receiving yards, and TD catches. In the pros, he became the first Lion receiver in eight years to make the Pro Bowl (2007).

■ **EARL CAMPBELL**, *Hall of Fame Running Back.* This 1977 Heisman Trophy–winning running back was picked first overall in the '78 draft by the Houston Oilers. He immediately dominated in the pros, winning both Rookie of the Year and MVP.

PENN STATE

Maurice Evans

A legendary coach keeps the Nittany Lions' winning tradition alive and well

One of the iconic images in sports is that of coach Joe Paterno prowling the sidelines at Penn State games in his familiar black sneakers and Coke-bottle eyeglasses. The 81-year-old Paterno has coached the Nittany Lions for 42 seasons, and the team has been a gridiron institution for nearly a century. Penn State holds the Division I record for most consecutive non-losing seasons (49) and has won four national championships. The Nittany Lions are ranked sixth in FBS history on the all-time wins list (789). Only Alabama and USC have more bowl game victories than their 26.

SCHOOL STATS
- **First Year:** 1887
- **National Championships:** 4
- **Bowl Appearances:** 40
- **All-Time Record:** 789–347–41
- **NFL Players Produced:** 309

PLAYERS TO WATCH IN 2008

■ MAURICE EVANS,

Junior, Defensive End, 6' 2", 264 lbs.
Evans is on the preseason Watch List for the Bronko Nagurski Trophy, which goes to the nation's best defender. Last season, he had 12.5 sacks, eighth-most in the nation. He was also a first-team All-Big Ten selection and a finalist for the Ted Hendricks Defensive End Award.

■ A.Q. SHIPLEY,

Senior, Center, 6' 1", 297 lbs. Voted a co-captain for the 2008 season by his teammates, Shipley is on the preseason watch list for the Rimington Trophy, which is awarded to the best center in the nation. He is also a leading candidate for the Lombardi Award (nation's best lineman) and the Outland Trophy (nation's best interior lineman).

▶ DERRICK WILLIAMS,

Senior, Wide Receiver, 6', 194 lbs. Williams is a cool customer both on and off the field. On the field, he is a shifty open-field runner with breakaway speed. Last season, he caught 55 passes for 529 yards, averaged 6.3 yards per rush, and had one punt return for a TD. Off the field, his easygoing personality made him the first freshman in many years to be allowed to talk with the media.

PENN STATE HISTORY
Paterno and the Nittany Lions Make Pennsylvania Proud

Located in the middle of Pennsylvania, Penn State is the center of the state's enormous football fan base. In 1911, the school won the first of back-to-back national championships. In 1967, one season after Joe Paterno was named coach, the Nittany Lions began a 30-game unbeaten streak that lasted until the 1970 season. Penn State would win national titles again in 1982 and '86. Still, the program's brightest moment came on October 27, 2001, when Paterno passed Alabama's Paul (Bear) Bryant to become the winningest coach in Division I-A history (324 wins).

TOP
NITTANY LIONS
IN THE
NFL

◀ **LARRY JOHNSON,** *Running Back, Kansas City Chiefs.* After being a backup for the first two seasons of his career, Johnson rushed for 1,750 yards in 2005. Since the 2005 season, he ranks second in the NFL in rushing yards (4,098) and rushing touchdowns (40).

■ **ROBBIE GOULD,** *Kicker, Chicago Bears.* Gould was a first-team All-Pro and a Pro Bowler in 2006. He leads all kickers in field goals made (63) over the past two seasons.

■ **FRANCO HARRIS,** *Hall of Fame Running Back.* When he retired in 1984, Harris ranked third in league history in rushing yards (12,120) and net yardage (14,622). He won four Super Bowls with the Pittsburgh Steelers, including Super Bowl IX, in which he was named MVP.

LSU

Is another title within grasp for the reigning national champions?

There's nothing more intimidating in college football than a night game at LSU's Tiger Stadium, known as Death Valley. With 92,400 screaming fans, many visiting teams have melted under the pressure in Baton Rouge, Louisiana. LSU is the only school to win two national championships under the Bowl Championship Series (BCS) format since it began in 1998. The defending national champions have won four national titles, and they rank in the Top 12 in FBS history in games won and bowl appearances.

Tyson Jackson

SCHOOL STATS
- **First Year:** 1893
- **National Championships:** 4
- **Bowl Appearances:** 39
- **All-Time Record:** 692–390–49
- **NFL Players Produced:** 252

PLAYERS TO WATCH IN 2008

◄ DEMETRIUS BYRD, *Senior, Wide Receiver, 6'2", 195 lbs.* Byrd is a big-play receiver who has been timed at 4.3 seconds in the 40-yard dash. A junior college transfer, he led the Tigers in touchdown catches (7) and was second in receiving yards (621) in 2007. Byrd averaged 17.7 yards per catch and had one touchdown catch in the SEC Championship Game.

■ TYSON JACKSON, *Senior, Defensive End, 6'5", 292 lbs.* ESPN analyst Kirk Herbstreit called Jackson a "defensive freak" because of his size, strength, and quickness. Last season, he led the Tigers in quarterback hurries (15) and

was second in pass breakups (10). In three seasons, he has 14 career sacks and 16.5 tackles for loss.

■ RICKY JEAN-FRANCOIS, *Junior, Defensive Tackle, 6'3", 281 lbs.* Jean-Francois will pick right up where 2008 first-round NFL draft pick Glenn Dorsey left off, carrying on LSU's tradition of great defensive tackles. He is on the Preseason Watch List for the 2008 Outland Trophy, which is awarded to the best interior lineman in the nation. In last season's national championship game, he blocked a field goal attempt and was named the game's outstanding defensive player.

LSU HISTORY

Earthshaking Success

Since its first game in 1893, LSU has had its share of unforgettable moments. Billy Cannon's fourth-quarter punt return, which led Number 1 LSU to victory over Number 3 Ole Miss on October 31, 1959, is called the Halloween Run. With the Tigers down 7–3 late in the fourth quarter, Cannon fielded a punt at his 11-yard line and avoided seven would-be tacklers as he danced down the right sideline for a touchdown. He won the Heisman Trophy that season. On October 8, 1988, the 79,341 fans in Tiger Stadium literally made the earth shake. When LSU scored a late touchdown to beat Auburn, Death Valley erupted and a seismograph in the LSU Geology Department registered a tremor. In front of the largest crowd in Tiger Stadium history last season, coach Les Miles earned a reputation for being a risk-taker. With top-ranked LSU losing by 10 points to Florida in the fourth quarter, Miles went for it on three fourth-down plays during two touchdown drives. The Tigers came back to win, 28–24.

TOP TIGERS IN THE NFL

▲ JOSEPH ADDAI, *Running Back, Indianapolis Colts.* In 2007, the versatile Addai tied for second in the NFL in rushing touchdowns (12) and touchdown catches among running backs (3). He has rushed for at least 1,000 yards in each of his first two pro seasons.

■ DWAYNE BOWE, *Wide Receiver, Kansas City Chiefs.* Bowe, the Chiefs' first round pick in 2007, led all rookie receivers in receptions (70), receiving yards (995), and receiving touchdowns (5) last season.

■ Y.A. TITTLE, *Hall of Fame Quarterback.* Tittle passed for 28,339 yards and 212 TD passes in 15 seasons. In 1963, he tied the NFL single-season record for TD passes (36) and was named league MVP.

FLORIDA

A high-octane offense has made the Gators a national power

Always one of the toughest teams in the SEC, the Gators feature an amazing offense. Since 1996, they have averaged a whopping 431.2 yards a game, best in the SEC. In 2007, Florida celebrated its 100th anniversary of football by winning its second national championship in school history. They have die-hard fans too. Ben Hill Griffin Stadium, known as The Swamp, is one of the toughest places to play. The Gators have lost only one home game in the past three seasons.

Tim Tebow

SCHOOL STATS

- **First Year:** 1906
- **National Championships:** 2
- **Bowl Appearances:** 35
- **All-Time Record:** 628–372–40
- **NFL Players Produced:** 240

PLAYERS TO WATCH IN 2008

◀ **PERCY HARVIN,**
Junior, Wide Receiver, 5' 11", 178 lbs.
Harvin is a receiver who often lines up in the backfield. In just two seasons, he already has the most career yards rushing by a Florida wide receiver (1,192). He is the only player in school history to have 100 yards rushing and receiving in a game. In 2007, he was second in the SEC in receiving yards per game (78) and was named a first team All-America by *The Sporting News.*

■ **TIM TEBOW,**
Junior, Quarterback, 6' 3", 235 lbs. Tebow is the ultimate dual-threat quarterback. He started all 13 games as a freshman and ran the top-ranked offense in the SEC, which averaged 42.5 points and 457.2 yards a game. In his second season, he led Florida in rushing with 895 yards and 23 touchdowns while completing 66.9 percent of his passes for 3,286 yards and 32 TDs. He capped it off by becoming the first sophomore in NCAA history to win the Heisman Trophy.

■ **BRANDON SPIKES,**
Junior, Linebacker, 6' 3", 243 lbs.
Spikes led the Gators with 131 total tackles, the second-most in the SEC. He also led the team and tied for third in the SEC in fumble recoveries (3), including two in a 51–31 victory over South Carolina. In 2007, he had at least three solo tackles in every game.

TOP GATORS IN THE NFL

▶ **FRED TAYLOR,** *Running Back, Jacksonville, Jaguars.* Taylor ranks fourth on Florida's all-time rushing list with 3,075 yards. He is second among active NFL running backs with 10,715 rushing yards.

■ **JEVON KEARSE,** *Defensive End, Tennessee Titans.* Kearse was an All-America at linebacker and he had 145 tackles, 16.5 sacks, and 6 forced fumbles from 1996 thorugh '98. In the pros, Kearse led his team in sacks in six of his first seven NFL seasons.

■ **JACK YOUNGBLOOD,** *Hall of Fame Defensive End.* Youngblood played 14 seasons for the Los Angeles Rams, which included a team-record 201 consecutive games. He was an All-Pro five times and played in seven straight Pro Bowls from 1973 through '79.

FLORIDA HISTORY
A Star Player Returns to Lead the Gators as a Coach
The Gators had some success in their early years, but started to dominate in the mid-1960s under coach Ray Graves. One of the most successful teams of that era was the 1966 squad led by Heisman-winning quarterback Steve Spurrier. Spurrier led the Gators to a 9–2 record and a win over Georgia Tech in the Orange Bowl that season. He returned to Florida as head coach in 1990. In 12 seasons, Spurrier coached the Gators to a 122–27–1 record, 11 bowl games, six SEC championships, and one national championship (1996). The University of Florida is also the birthplace of Gatorade, which was invented for Gator football players when their coaches became concerned that the athletes would become dehydrated in the intense heat.

TENNESSEE

An SEC crown is always within reach for the pride of the Volunteer state

Check out this list of accomplishments: The ninth-most wins of any program in college football history, the fourth-most bowl victories, regular finishes at the top of the SEC standings, two national titles, and a group of grads that includes one of the NFL's all-time great quarterbacks. Not bad, eh? The Volunteers have won nearly 70 percent of their games while competing in the always tough SEC. And with most of last year's SEC East division championship team returning, Tennessee has the makings of a Top 10 team in 2008.

Arian Foster

SCHOOL STATS

- **First Year:** 1891
- **National Championships:** 2
- **Bowl Appearances:** 47
- **All-Time Record:** 771-320-53
- **NFL Players Produced:** 286

PLAYERS TO WATCH IN 2008

◀ **ERIC BERRY,**
Sophomore, Defensive Back, 5' 11", 195 lbs.
Berry earned freshman All-America honors and was named the top freshman defender in the SEC. He intercepted a team-high five passes in 2007. Berry might even get some time at quarterback in '08.

■ **ARIAN FOSTER,**
Senior, Running Back, 6' 1", 215 lbs. Foster is on pace to finish his career as Tennessee's all-time leading rusher. He is just 685 yards shy of the record (3,078). In 2005, Foster became the first Tennessee freshman to start at tailback since Jamal Lewis in 1997. Last season, he finished third in the SEC in rushing yards (1,193) and tied for fifth in total TDs (14). He earned second-team all-SEC honors. With QB Erik Ainge gone to the NFL, Foster will be asked to carry an even heavier load in 2008.

■ **DANIEL LINCOLN,**
Sophomore, Kicker, 6', 204 lbs. Lincoln's 115 points were the most by a kicker in Vols history. The Football Writers Association of America named him an All-America after he made 21 of 29 field goal attempts in '07.

TOP VOLUNTEERS IN THE NFL

▶ **PEYTON MANNING,** *Quarterback, Indianapolis Colts.* A three-time All-America at Tennessee, Manning is a two-time NFL MVP, six-time All-Pro selection, and was MVP of Super Bowl XLI. He has started all 160 games since entering the league in 1998, when the Colts made him the Number 1 pick of the draft.

■ **JOHN HENDERSON,** *Defensive Tackle, Jacksonville Jaguars.* A two-time All-America and the 2000 Outland Trophy winner (nation's best interior lineman) for the Vols, Henderson made the Pro Bowl in 2004 and '06. He is a top-notch run stuffer and has 24 sacks in six NFL seasons.

■ **REGGIE WHITE,** *Hall of Fame Defensive End.* Still Tennessee's all-time sack leader (32), White went on to become one of the NFL's all-time greatest pass rushers for the Eagles, Packers, and Panthers from 1985 through 2000. The Minister of Defense had 198 sacks and was twice named Defensive Player of the Year.

TENNESSEE HISTORY
From Pickup Football to Big-Time Football

Tennessee football started as a ragtag group of students who got together to play informally in 1891. But the Vols gradually improved. And when legendary coach Robert Neyland took over the program in 1926, they transformed into one of the nation's best teams. Tennessee won its first conference title in 1930. The Vols went undefeated in the regular season from 1938 through '40. The '39 team was the last in NCAA history to go the entire regular season without allowing a point. They won their first consensus national title in 1951, and Neyland retired after the '52 season. It took the Vols 47 years to win their next national title. Led by QB Tee Martin and linebacker Al Wilson, the Vols went 13-0, upsetting Florida State in the Fiesta Bowl to win the BCS championship in 1998.

WEST VIRGINIA

With an unstoppable ground game, the Mountaineers keep climbing to new heights

Noel Devine

West Virginia is the best college football program to have never won a national championship. The Mountaineers have 664 wins, the 15th most of any school, and have won four of the past five Big East titles. The school has been in the national title hunt in each of the past three seasons. West Virginia and USC are the only two schools to have played in BCS bowl games in each of the past five years.

SCHOOL STATS

- **First Year:** 1891
- **NCAA Championships:** 0
- **Bowl Appearances:** 27
- **All-Time Record:** 664–442–45
- **NFL Players Produced:** 157

PLAYERS TO WATCH IN 2008

■ REED WILLIAMS,
Senior, Linebacker, 6'2", 225 lbs.
The linebacker led the Mountaineers with 107 tackles last season. He won the 2008 Tostitos Fiesta Bowl Defensive MVP award.

■ NOEL DEVINE,
Sophomore, Running Back, 5'8", 173 lbs.
With star running back Steve Slaton now in the NFL, Devine will get the starting nod in '08. He was third on the team with 627 yards and averaged 8.6 yards per carry last season.

▶ PAT WHITE,
Senior, Quarterback, 6'1", 192 lbs.
One of the greatest rushing quarterbacks in NCAA history, White returns to WVU for his senior season. He already has more rushing yards (3,506) than any other QB in Big East history. In 2007, he had 3,059 total yards and 28 touchdowns. In his career, he has rushed for 100 yards in 15 games and 200 yards in three games.

TOP MOUNTAINEERS IN THE NFL

■ **SAM HUFF**, *Hall of Fame linebacker.* The 6'1", 230-pound Huff dominated from 1956 through '69 for the New York Giants and Washington Redskins. He was named to three NFL All-Pro teams and was known for his hard hits on opposing running backs.

▲ **MARC BULGER**, *Quarterback, St. Louis Rams.* Bulger has led the Rams' high-flying offense since 2002. He has a strong arm, but has had injury problems throughout his career. He has been dominant when he has played. Bulger's best season was 2006 when he played 16 games and threw for 4,301 yards.

■ **MIKE VANDERJAGT**, *Former Dallas Cowboys kicker.* Vanderjagt is the most accurate kicker in NFL history. In his 10-season career with the Indianapolis Colts and Dallas Cowboys, he made 86.5 percent of his kicks.

WVU HISTORY
A Rat Starts a Winning Trend
Mountaineer football didn't get off to the best start. In its first game, on Thanksgiving Day 1891, West Virginia lost to Washington & Jefferson College, 72–0. West Virginia continued to struggle until 1915, when fullback Ira Errett (Rat) Rodgers emerged as a star. How good was Rodgers? He scored all 147 of the team's points in 1919 and led the Mountaineers to a win over powerful Princeton that year. In his three seasons with WVU, the squad was 24–8–4. The Mountaineers had up-and-down teams until the early 1980s, when they became a force under coach Don Nehlen. The '88 squad nearly won the national championship, losing its only game to Notre Dame in the Fiesta Bowl. Coach Rich Rodriguez kept WVU on top after he took over for Nehlen in '01. The team had three straight double-digit win seasons from '05 through '07. Rodriguez left to coach Michigan in January, and new coach Bill Stewart will try to continue the Mountaineers' recent run of success.

AUBURN

The Tigers are a dominant — and often overlooked — program

Auburn is known for producing consistently competitive teams and top-notch players. The school has won one national championship and 10 conference titles (six since they joined the always-tough SEC), and 62 Tigers have made All-America teams. Much of Auburn's success has come recently. They are one of only nine programs to have won more than 70 percent of their games over the past 25 seasons. The Tigers are also one of only two FBS programs (along with Nebraska) to go perfect more than once in the past 15 seasons. They were undefeated and untied in 1993 and again in 2004.

Antonio Coleman

SCHOOL STATS
- **First Year:** 1892
- **National Championships:** 1
- **Bowl Appearances:** 34
- **All-Time Record:** 676–388–47
- **NFL Players Produced:** 214

PLAYERS TO WATCH IN 2008

◀ **RODGERIQUS SMITH,** *Senior, Wide Receiver, 6', 188 lbs.* Smith will be the Tigers' top receiver again this season. With 1,266 career receiving yards, he is 14th on Auburn's all-time list. Smith is 734 yards shy of becoming the fifth player in Auburn history with 2,000 or more receiving yards. He has made at least one catch in 24 consecutive games, and has led Auburn in touchdown receptions in each of the past two seasons. His 705 receiving yards in 2007 were 10th-best in the SEC.

■ **ANTONIO COLEMAN,** *Junior, Defensive End, 6' 2", 243 lbs.* Coleman made his presence known as an edge pass rusher last season. In his first year as a starter, he finished tied for fifth in the SEC with 8.5 sacks and was fourth in the SEC with 18.5 tackles for loss.

■ **SEN'DERRICK MARKS,** *Junior, Defensive End, 6' 1", 291 lbs.* Marks is a big reason the Tigers aren't too worried about star defensive tackle Pat Sims entering the NFL a year early. A freakish athlete for his size, Marks is being billed as a future first-round pick himself. The All-America candidate has started every game for the Tigers the past two seasons. He had 43 tackles last year.

TOP TIGERS IN THE NFL

AUBURN HISTORY
Two Undefeated Seasons Without a Championship

Auburn's first official head coach was John Heisman, who later had the sport's most famous trophy named after him. Heisman coached the Tigers from 1895–99, going 12-4-2. Led by All-America end Jimmy Phillips, the Tigers took home their only national title in 1957. In 1971, star quarterback Pat Sullivan won the program's first Heisman Trophy. In '93, the team was shut out of bowl contention because of NCAA sanctions, but new coach Terry Bowden led the Tigers to an 11-0 record. Their win streak ran to 20, a program record, the next season. Still, the Tigers' 2004 team might have been the best of all. Auburn went 13-0, led by future NFL stars Carlos Rogers, Jason Campbell, Cadillac Williams, and Ronnie Brown. However, they were shut out of the national championship game again because of the BCS system.

▶ **JASON CAMPBELL,** *Quarterback, Washington Redskins.* The SEC Offensive Player of the Year in 2004, Campbell was taken with the 25th pick of the '05 Draft. He threw for 2,700 yards in '07 despite missing the final three games with a left knee injury.

■ **KARLOS DANSBY,** *Linebacker, Arizona Cardinals.* An All-America for the Tigers in 2003, Dansby led the Cardinals with 99 tackles last season. Since entering the NFL, he is the only player in the league with more than 250 solo tackles and 20 sacks.

■ **BO JACKSON,** *Legendary running back.* The 1985 Heisman Trophy winner was drafted Number 1 in the '86 NFL Draft, but chose to play baseball instead (he was the MVP of the '89 All-Star game). In '87, the Raiders re-drafted him with the promise that he could play both sports. Jackson made the Pro Bowl in '90, but his career was cut short by a hip injury.

TEXAS A&M

Texas's _other_ college power has carved out a proud history of its own

Jorvorskie Lane

Texas A&M football is known for its "12th man," the nickname for the energetic students that cheer them on at Kyle Field. But over the years, it has been the 11 men they put on the field who have made the Aggies one of the nation's best. A&M won two national championships in the early days of college football and its 94 wins in the 1990s were second only to Nebraska among Big 12 teams. With former Green Bay Packers coach Mike Sherman now running the program, the Aggies are gearing up for a run back to the top.

SCHOOL STATS
- **First Year:** 1894
- **National Championships:** 2
- **Bowl Appearances:** 30
- **All-Time Record:** 655–425–48
- **NFL Players Produced:** 224

PLAYERS TO WATCH IN 2008

■ JORVORSKIE LANE,

Senior, Running Back, 6', 268 lbs. A big, bruising back, Lane tied for second in the Big 12 last season with 16 rushing touchdowns. New coach Mike Sherman will move Lane to fullback this season, where he'll serve primarily as a lead blocker.

■ MIKE GOODSON,

Junior, Running Back, 6', 206 lbs. After a promising freshman season in 2006 (847 rushing yards), Goodson took a back seat to Lane last year. He was third on the team with 711 rushing yards. But this year, Goodson is expected to be the focus of the offense since Lane is moving to fullback. With game-breaking speed, Goodson should easily surpass 1,000 yards in '08.

▶ STEPHEN McGEE,

Senior, Quarterback, 6'3", 220 lbs. McGee is one of college football's top dual-threat quarterbacks. In 2007, he was one of six players in Division I with more than 2,000 passing yards (2,311) and 800 rushing yards (899). He led the Aggies in both categories. McGee had four 100-yard rushing games, but the season's highlight was A&M's upset over Texas. In that game, McGee had a career-high 362 passing yards, three passing touchdowns, and a rushing TD. In '06, he set the Aggies' single-season record by completing 62 percent of his passes.

TOP AGGIES IN THE NFL

▶ **SHANE LECHLER,** *Punter, Oakland Raiders.* A two-time All-America at A&M, Lechler has become arguably the greatest punter of all-time. His career 46.5 yard per punt average is the highest in NFL history, and he has made five All-Pro teams.

■ **Pat Williams,** *Defensive Tackle, Minnesota Vikings.* A second-team All-Southwest Conference selection as a junior in '95, Williams is now one of the NFL's premiere run stuffers. He was selected to the Pro Bowl in 2006 and '07.

■ **LESTER HAYES,** *Legendary Cornerback.* An All-America safety for the Aggies, Hayes went on to become one of the NFL's all-time great corners. He popularized the physical coverage style called "bump and run." Hayes was a four-time All-Pro selection for the Oakland Raiders and was the NFL Defensive Player of the Year in 1980.

TEXAS A&M HISTORY

Coach X Marks the Spot

Head coach Dana X. Bible brought a series of firsts to the Aggies. The Hall of Fame coach led A&M to its first conference title in 1917 (they played in the Southwest Conference), finishing with a perfect 8-0 record. Two years later, the Aggies won a share of their first national title with a 10-0 season. And in 1921, A&M's Lone Star showdown game against rival Texas became the first college football game to be broadcast live on the radio. Bible left for Nebraska after the 1928 season, but another Hall of Fame coach, Homer Norton, led A&M to its only outright title in 1939. Running back John David Crow became the school's only Heisman winner in 1957. A&M won its lone Big 12 title in 1998, thanks to a suffocating defense led by linebacker Dat Nguyen.

GEORGIA

A strong tradition has made this school a Top Dog in the South

With more than 700 all-time victories and two **Heisman Trophy winners**, Georgia football can measure up to just about any other program. The Bulldogs have one national championship, 12 SEC titles, four undefeated seasons, 66 All-America players, and 11 College Football Hall of Fame inductees. And with a 64–15 record over the past six seasons and plenty of stars returning from a team that finished ranked Number 2 in the AP Poll last year, it looks like they are ready to take over at the top.

Geno Atkins

SCHOOL STATS
- **First Year:** 1892
- **National Championships:** 1
- **Bowl Appearances:** 43
- **All-Time Record:** 713–381–54
- **NFL Players Produced:** 233

PLAYERS TO WATCH IN 2008

■ **GENO ATKINS,**
Junior, Defensive Tackle, 6' 1", 290 lbs.
One of the most disruptive interior linemen in the nation, Atkins was a first-team all-SEC selection last season. He led Georgia with 14.5 tackles for loss.

■ **MATTHEW STAFFORD,**
Junior, Quarterback, 6' 3", 237 lbs.
Stafford has one of the nation's strongest arms. He finished in the SEC's top five in passing yards (2,523) and TDs (19). Going into the season, Stafford was touted as the possible top overall pick of the 2009 NFL Draft if he leaves college after this season.

▶ **KNOWSHON MORENO,**
Sophomore, Running Back, 5' 11", 207 lbs.
In 2007, Moreno's rushing total (1,334 yards) was the second-highest in school history and fourth-best in Southeastern Conference history for a freshman. Moreno also tied for third in the conference with 14 rushing TDs and was named the SEC Freshman of the Year. With his ability to out-run defenders or power through them, Moreno will be the key to the offense again this season. In May, SI.com ranked him the Number 3 contender for the 2008 Heisman Trophy, behind '07 winner Tim Tebow of Florida and Ohio State running back Chris Wells.

TOP BULLDOGS IN THE NFL

▶ **HINES WARD**, *Wide Receiver, Pittsburgh Steelers.* A star receiver, tailback, and quarterback for the 'Dawgs, Ward has gone on to make four NFL Pro Bowls. He was MVP of Super Bowl XL and is Pittsburgh's all-time leader in receptions (719), TD catches (65), and receiving yards (8,737).

■ **CHAMP BAILEY**, *Cornerback, Denver Broncos.* The 1998 Nagurski Award winner as the nation's best defensive player, Bailey is now considered the best cover man in the NFL. He has been selected to eight Pro Bowls for the Redskins and Broncos.

■ **FRAN TARKENTON**, *Hall of Fame Quarterback.* Tarkenton led Georgia to the 1959 SEC title and was famous for avoiding pass rushers with his scrambling ability. In the NFL, he led the Vikings to three Super Bowls and was the league's MVP in 1975.

GEORGIA HISTORY
The Good Ol' (Dog) Days

Georgia nearly played its final game in 1897. The state wanted to ban football after fullback Von Gammon died from injuries sustained in a game. But Governor William Yates Atkinson vetoed the bill because of an appeal by Gammon's mother, and the Bulldogs played on. The program rose to the top in the 1920s, with the team going a perfect 8-0 in 1920 and 9-1 in '27. Star halfback Frank Sinkwich became the SEC's first Heisman Trophy winner in 1942. He led the team to an 11-1 record, a Rose Bowl win over UCLA, and the Number 1 ranking in several polls. Great seasons followed, but it wasn't until 1980 that Georgia claimed its first official national title under legendary coach Vince Dooley and freshman running back Herschel Walker. Walker set the NCAA freshman rushing record, and the Bulldogs went 12-0, beating Notre Dame in the Sugar Bowl.

BYU

The Cougars are on the verge of joining the traditional college football big shots

Jan
Jorgensen

The BYU Cougars are proof that you don't have to be in a **BCS** conference to be a college football powerhouse. The team from Provo, Utah has crashed the big-conference party often, winning a national title in 1984 and then boasting a Heisman-winner in Ty Detmer six seasons later. The Cougars narrowly missed making a BCS bowl in two of the past seven seasons. Prospects are bright for 2008. Ten of 11 starters are returning on offense, and the Cougars own the longest winning streak in all of Division I. They won their 10th straight game when they beat UCLA in the Las Vegas Bowl, 17–16, last December.

SCHOOL STATS

- **First Year:** 1922
- **National Championships:** 1
- **Bowl Appearances:** 26
- **All-Time Record:** 485–369–26
- **NFL Players Produced:** 130

PLAYERS TO WATCH IN 2008

◄ **HARVEY UNGA,** *Sophomore, Running Back, 6', 243 lbs.* A big, versatile back, Unga was named the Mountain West Conference Freshman of the Year and earned Freshman All-America honors in 2007. He set conference freshman records for rushing yards (1,227) and yards from scrimmage (1,840), and led the Mountain West with 17 touchdowns. Unga also led all MWC freshmen in catches (44) and receiving yards (655). In 2008, he will be a candidate for the Doak Walker Award, given to the nation's best running back.

■ **JAN JORGENSEN,** *Junior, Defensive End, 6'3", 256 lbs.* Jorgensen was first-team all-MWC last season and led the conference with 14 sacks. He was also a force against the run, finishing twelfth in FBS and had a conference-best 20 tackles for loss.

■ **MAX HALL,** *Junior, Quarterback, 6'1", 201 lbs.* Hall should be a Heisman candidate in 2008. After transferring from Arizona State in 2006, he finished ninth in the nation with 3,848 passing yards and led the Mountain West with 26 touchdown passes in '07. He was named first-team all-conference.

TOP COUGARS IN THE NFL

► **BRADY POPPINGA,** *Linebacker, Green Bay Packers.* A three-time all-conference player at BYU, Poppinga is entering his third season as a starting LB for the Packers. He had 88 tackles over the past two seasons.

■ **JOHN TAIT,** *Offensive Tackle, Chicago Bears.* An All-America during his senior season at BYU, the Chiefs made Tait the 14th pick of the 1999 draft. He's been a starter each of the past eight seasons.

■ **STEVE YOUNG,** *Hall of Fame Quarterback.* An All-America for the Cougars in 1983, Young's NFL career took off when he became the San Francisco 49ers starter in '91. Young went on to win two NFL MVP Awards and was MVP of Super Bowl XXIX. His career passer rating of 96.8 is the highest all time.

BYU HISTORY

"QB U" Flies High With an Awesome Aerial Attack

The Cougars didn't exactly get off to a roaring start. The football program began in 1922, but didn't win a conference title until 1965. That season, quarterback Virgil Carter led BYU to the Western Athletic Conference championship. But the program didn't really take off until LaVell Edwards became coach in 1972 and installed a pass-happy offense. From 1976–85, BYU won 10 straight WAC titles. After star QB Steve Young graduated in 1983, Robbie Bosco led the Cougars to the 1984 national championship and a 13–0 record. In 1990, Ty Detmer won the first Heisman for "QB U." Detmer threw for a then-NCAA record 5,188 yards, and led BYU to an upset win over top-ranked Miami early in the season. BYU joined the new Mountain West Conference in 1999. Edwards retired after the 2000 season, finishing with 20 conference championships.

VIRGINIA TECH

The Hokies have been bowl-bound for 15 years and counting

Under coach Frank Beamer, the Hokies have become a force in the ACC. Virginia Tech is one of four FBS schools to play in a bowl game in each of the past 15 seasons. They have had at least 10 wins in each of the past four seasons, and are coming off their second ACC championship and a berth in the Orange Bowl.

Kam Chancellor

SCHOOL STATS
- **First Year:** 1992
- **National Championships:** 0
- **Bowl Appearances:** 21
- **All-Time Record:** 647–421–46
- **NFL Players Produced:** 130

PLAYERS TO WATCH IN 2008

◀ SEAN GLENNON,

Senior, Quarterback, 6'4", 223 lbs. Glennon has had an up-and-down career at Tech. He won the starting QB job as a sophomore in 2006, and became the seventh Hokie signal-caller to pass for at least 2,000 yards in a season. He struggled early in 2007, and was replaced by freshman Tyrod Taylor. When Taylor got hurt in the seventh game, Glennon came back and finished second in the ACC in passer efficiency (137.6). He was also named MVP of the ACC championship game after throwing for 174 yards and three touchdowns.

■ ORION MARTIN,

Senior, Defensive End, 6'2", 252 lbs. Martin is the only returning Hokie defensive lineman to have started every game last season. He was second on the team with 6.5 sacks. His younger brother, Cam, is a starting linebacker for Tech.

■ KAM CHANCELLOR,

Junior, Safety, 6'3", 225 lbs. Chancellor was a starter at rover last season, but will play free safety in 2008. He was tied for fourth on the team with 79 tackles and will be counted on as a defensive leader this year.

VIRGINIA TECH HISTORY

Fashionably Late to the BCS Party

The Hokies are newbies to the college football power structure. The school has fielded a football team since 1892, but didn't become major players on the national scene until Frank Beamer took over as coach in 1987. Fifteen of Virginia Tech's 21 bowl appearances have come since 1993. The school had its best team in 1999, led by quarterback Michael Vick. The sophomore carried the Hokies to the national championship game, and the team nearly upset heavily favored Florida State in the Sugar Bowl. Since then, Virginia Tech has made a BCS Bowl two more times.

TOP HOKIES IN THE NFL

▲ **SHAYNE GRAHAM,** *Kicker, Cincinnati Bengals.* Graham is second on the NFL's all-time list for career field-goal accuracy. He has made 85.39 percent of his kicks in eight seasons with Cincinnati.

■ **KEVIN JONES,** *Former Detroit Lions Running Back.* A first-team All-America at Tech, Jones has been a terrific weapon as a rusher and receiver out of the backfield in the NFL. His problem has been staying healthy. He has missed at least three games in each of the past three seasons.

■ **BRUCE SMITH,** *Legendary Defensive End.* An unstoppable pass rusher, the 6'4", 262-pound end made the Pro Bowl 11 times in his 19 seasons with the Buffalo Bills and Washington Redskins. His 200 career sacks are the most in NFL history.

SMALL CONFEREN

DIVISION I FOOTBALL CHAMPIONSHIP SERIES
APPALACHIAN STATE ▶

The Mountaineers won their third straight national championship in 2007, but that title didn't get nearly the attention of their first game of the season. Appalachian State pulled off one of the biggest upsets in college football history when it beat Michigan, 34–32, last September. Prospects for a fourth straight title are looking good with junior quarterback Armanti Edwards behind center. Last season, Edwards had six games with more than 100 yards passing and rushing. On November 3, he had 291 yards rushing against The Citadel. The following week, he had 295 yards passing against Western Carolina.

Armanti Edwards

Brad Iciek

DIVISION II
◀ GRAND VALLEY STATE

How's this for dominance? The Lakers have gone 91–6 in their last 97 games. Since 2001, the school has made it to five national championship games, winning four of them. Grand Valley State's loss to Northwest Missouri State in the 2007 Division II semifinals snapped the Lakers' 40-game winning streak. With junior quarterback Brad Iciek running the offense in 2008, GVS will surely be in the title hunt once agan.

DIVISION III
MOUNT UNION ▶

Since 1996, Mount Union has won eight Division III national championships. Running back Nate Kmic had 1,700 yards rushing with 38 touchdowns last season. In the first quarter of the Purple Raiders' game against Averett last September, Kmic scored four TDs. Mount Union scored a record 52 points in the first quarter of that game.

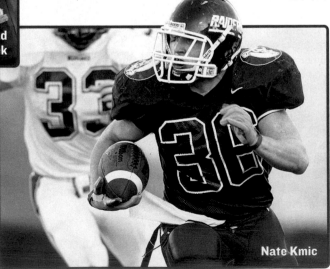

Nate Kmic

CE POWERS

SMALL SCHOOL STARS IN THE NFL

These guys didn't play Division I-A football, but still became big-time players in the pros

▶ Jerry Rice
Wide Receiver, Mississippi Valley State
The greatest wide receiver in history made the Pro Bowl 13 times and holds nearly every major NFL receiving record. He helped the San Francisco 49ers win three Super Bowls from 1988 through 1994.

▲ Brian Westbrook
Running Back, Villanova
Westbrook has become one of the NFL's best all-around backs. In 2007, he led the NFL in yards from scrimmage (2,104) and set the Philadelphia Eagles franchise reception record (90).

▶ Walter Payton
Running Back, Jackson State
Payton won the rushing title and was named the NFL MVP in 1977. He finished his career as the NFL's all-time leader in total yards (21,264) and rushing touchdowns (110).

◀ Michael Strahan
Defensive End, Texas Southern
The New York Giants end is one of the greatest pass rushers of all time. He holds the NFL record for sacks in a season (22.5) and is the active leader in career sacks (141.5).

▲ Darren Sharper
Safety, William & Mary
Sharper is a leader on the Minnesota Vikings' stingy defense. His 51 interceptions and 954 interception return yards since 1998 are the most of any NFL player.

DIVISION I
FOOTBALL BOWL SUBDIVISION (FBS)

ATLANTIC COAST CONFERENCE
Boston College Eagles
Clemson Tigers
Duke Blue Devils
Florida State Seminoles
Georgia Tech Yellow Jackets
Maryland Terrapins
Miami (Florida) Hurricanes
North Carolina State Wolfpack
North Carolina Tar Heels
Virginia Cavaliers
Virginia Tech Hokies
Wake Forest Demon Deacons

BIG 12
Baylor Bears
Colorado Buffaloes
Iowa State Cyclones
Kansas Jayhawks
Kansas State Wildcats
Missouri Tigers
Nebraska Cornhuskers
Oklahoma Sooners
Oklahoma State Cowboys
Texas Longhorns
Texas A&M Aggies
Texas Tech Red Raiders

BIG EAST
Cincinnati Bearcats
Connecticut Huskies
Louisville Cardinals
Pittsburgh Panthers
Rutgers Scarlet Knights
South Florida Bulls
Syracuse Orange
West Virginia Mountaineers

BIG TEN
Illinois Fighting Illini
Indiana Hoosiers
Iowa Hawkeyes
Michigan Wolverines
Michigan State Spartans
Minnesota Golden Gophers
Northwestern Wildcats
Ohio State Buckeyes
Penn State Nittany Lions
Purdue Boilermakers
Wisconsin Badgers

CONFERENCE USA
East Carolina Pirates
Houston Cougars
Marshall Thundering Herd
Memphis Tigers
Rice Owls
SMU Mustangs
Southern Miss Golden Eagles
Texas-El Paso Miners
Tulane Green Wave
Tulsa Golden Hurricane
UAB Blazers
UCF Knights

INDEPENDENT
Army Black Knights
Navy Midshipmen
Notre Dame Fighting Irish
Western Kentucky Hilltoppers

MID-AMERICAN
Akron Zips
Ball State Cardinals
Bowling Green Falcons
Buffalo Bulls
Central Michigan Chippewas
Eastern Michigan Eagles
Kent State Golden Flashes
Miami (Ohio) RedHawks
Northern Illinois Huskies
Ohio University Bobcats
Temple Owls
Toledo Rockets
Western Michigan Broncos

MOUNTAIN WEST
Air Force Falcons
BYU Cougars
Colorado State Rams
New Mexico Lobos
San Diego State Aztecs
TCU Horned Frogs
UNLV Rebels
Utah Utes
Wyoming Cowboys

PACIFIC 10
Arizona Wildcats
Arizona State Sun Devils
California Golden Bears
Oregon Ducks
Oregon State Beavers
Stanford Cardinal
UCLA Bruins
USC Trojans
Washington Huskies
Washington State Cougars

SOUTHEASTERN
Alabama Crimson Tide
Arkansas Razorbacks
Auburn Tigers
Florida Gators
Georgia Bulldogs
Kentucky Wildcats
LSU Tigers
Mississippi State Bulldogs
Ole Miss Rebels
South Carolina Gamecocks
Tennessee Volunteers
Vanderbilt Commodores

SUN BELT
Arkansas State Red Wolves
Florida Atlantic Owls
Florida Int'l Golden Panthers
Louisiana-Lafayette Ragin' Cajuns
Louisiana-Monroe Warhawks
Middle Tennessee Blue Raiders
North Texas Mean Green
Troy Trojans

WESTERN ATHLETIC
Boise State Broncos
Fresno State Bulldogs
Hawaii Warriors
Idaho Vandals
Louisiana Tech Bulldogs
Nevada Wolf Pack
New Mexico State Aggies
San Jose State Spartans
Utah State Aggies

TRIVIA

Ready to test your knowledge of college football? Try and tackle this quiz.

1) New York Knicks guard Nate Robinson played cornerback for which Division I program in 2002?
A. WASHINGTON
B. WISCONSIN
C. MICHIGAN

Nate Robinson

2) Which Division I school holds the record for most Rose Bowl appearances (32) and wins (23)?
A. MICHIGAN
B. USC
C. OHIO STATE

3) Which University of Hawaii quarterback set the NCAA record for career games with at least 400 yards passing (14), in 2006?
A. TIMMY CHANG
B. COLT BRENNAN
C. TY DETMER

4) The 2001 Miami Hurricanes had four future NFL running backs on their roster, including Willis McGahee, Clinton Portis, and Najeh Davenport. Who was the fourth?
A. EDGERRIN JAMES
B. FRANK GORE
C. LaMONT JORDAN

5) Which NFL superstar rushed for a Division I record 406 yards in a game for Texas Christian on November 20, 1999?
A. MARSHALL FAULK
B. EMMITT SMITH
C. LaDAINIAN TOMLINSON

6) What university had the longest winning streak in college football history, with 47 straight wins between 1953 and 1957?
A. OKLAHOMA
B. MICHIGAN
C. NOTRE DAME

7) Which school won the first recognized national championship in intercollegiate football history in 1869?
A. RUTGERS
B. PRINCETON
C. MICHIGAN

Clinton Portis

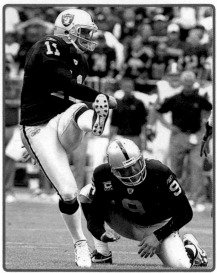

8) Which Florida State alum is the most recent kicker/punter to be drafted in the first round? Hint: He was drafted by the Oakland Raiders with the 17th pick in 2000 and is pictured above.
A. NATE KAEDING
B. SEBASTIAN JANIKOWSKI
C. JOSH BROWN

9) In 2006, which school became the first to win national championships in both football and basketball in the same year?
A. FLORIDA
B. OHIO STATE
C. MARYLAND

10) Which team upset Oklahoma in the Fiesta Bowl in 2007?
A. OHIO STATE
B. WEST VIRGINIA
C. BOISE STATE

48

ANSWERS: 1.A; 2.B; 3.B; 4.B; 5.C; 6.A; 7.B; 8.B; 9.A; 10.C